Poems For My Wife

Brick of Gold Publishing Company
New York
2020

For Shawna

I am not a romantic. I write short, funny poems. Then I met Shawna. We spent a night together. The next day, we took a road trip and swore we'd spend our lives together. I try to explain what happened in "Our Story", the longest and last poem in this book.

Two weeks later, I moved to Africa. I had accepted a job in Uganda, and had no choice but to say goodbye for nearly a year. It was hard. Our lives were disjointed. We spent hours on the phone. She was in Tennessee. I was ten thousand miles away. When I got time off, we met in Chicago, LA, New York, Florida, Nashville, Paris, Greece. One day we would be talking about the boring details of our lives over a bad internet connection. The next we would be in a hotel room or on a beach before saying goodbye again. We could not understand why we couldn't just be together. It did not feel like too much to ask for.

Many of the poems in this book are recollections from my bedroom in Africa of the days and nights and weeks we spent together touching, talking, planning our family and future. It is a gift, and a reminder - because Shawna has a bad memory (she is going to kill me for saying that), of our weird and thrilling and painful first year together, and apart.

I am still not a romantic. I do not believe everyone is destined to find true love or that distance makes the heart grow fonder or in many other popular sayings about love we often hear - in fact, the distance nearly killed us. But we got lucky, and I am a romantic for Shawna, at least. Whenever I get the chance, I dance with her and look into her big green eyes and ask her to marry me again, and again, and again.

We hope you get lucky too.

OUR WORLD

I will show you a world
You never knew was possible
And you will do the same
For me
And our love for each other
Will become love for all

NASHVILLE

We fell in love
In Nashville
In the parlor
Talking about gods and aliens
You wore a white tee shirt
And ripped jeans
With a scarf in your hair
You asked if I thought you were weird
I already knew
You were my wife

STILL

When you have tired yourself
I will carry you to new worlds
Sometimes you will be buried by unbreathable earth
And sometimes you will have no body
A single point in space
Full of light
Sometimes I will fuck you like an animal
From behind
In the kitchen
And you will know where your body is
And what it is for
And sometimes we will be still

LA

Animals
Hold the ledge
In the dark
In LA
Your whiskey shadow moves under us
I sink my heavy teeth into your shoulder
And surround you
And we know
Nothing else matters

CREAM

I will love you
In the mornings
And smile at you
And make you coffee
With cream in it
And we will sit and talk
And you will stop talking
When you realize I am not listening
Because I am thinking of how much I love you

YOU'LL NEVER KNOW

You'll never know
What you've done for me
I waited for you
For so long
I thought there was something wrong
And now you are here
And I am so happy

THE SHOWER

You get in first
To get wet
And smile when you see me
I wash you from behind
Suddenly you are as blind as any animal
That just wants to be fucked
And so am I

WEAK

I was so strong
It was just me
And everything else
I didn't need anyone
I welcomed death
Didn't welcome it
But didn't fear it
Found comfort in it
You made me weak
Now, it's me, you, and everything else
In that order
Or just me and you
Or you and everything and me
Somewhere
You made me human
I never want to leave
I want to wake up and search the covers for you
Every morning
And know you are there

SHINE

When I am with you
I don't have to talk
Or show off
I just want you to shine

PARIS

Remember our first dinner
In Paris
It rained
Cas' favorite restaurant was closed
Because it was August
So we went across the street
And sat at the little table in the doorway
And watched people in wet clothes with wet hair
Ride bikes over wet bridges

DIRTY

When I am alone
I think about
Before we go out
When you've just finished your hair
And makeup
And look in the mirror
One knee bent
Head tilted
Hands on your hips
Impressed by yourself
And see me
Behind you
And feel my arms
Around you

THE SPACE BETWEEN THINGS

I catch myself
Surprised I am alive
I feel air on my lips
I feel the space between things
And suddenly
Always
I think of you

PROVIDENCE

Pulling off the highway
Winding around and past a small bridge
I thought
What the fuck am I doing in Providence
Four and a half hours north
To see you
At a salon

THROUGH THE SKY

Things will change
And we will walk
Side by side
Through the sky
Together
Looking at the world
Through the same eyes

THE BAR

Last night
At the bar
I looked at you
You had the dumbest look on your face
And I loved it

IN THE END

I will die
And you will die
And in the end
Our love
Is all that matters

Poems For My Wife

IN YOU

Sometimes we speak plainly
We must live in the world
What else is there to do
But below the words
My love is in you

CHICAGO

Who was that Mike guy
Anyways
It was weird
At first
Like we didn't know each other
Then
We went to the Mexican place
Mike gave us a ride
Elliot was there
People gave us drinks
We felt like
We were floating
I'm not sure if it was the jetlag
Or being near you
But soon
Our hearts found our bodies

SWIRLING

Just before we fuck
Sometimes
For a moment
The world goes windless
Grass stands straight
Heads and ears lift
Until we set the world swirling
Again
With our love

ONE DAY

One day
You will look at me
With our baby boy or girl
And feel so much love
You will be stunned
And I will look at you
And smile
And take you into our bedroom
And fuck you

SURFACE

Somewhere a black ball spins
Pulling me up to you
To the surface
A thousand times
You are my Earth

UNAFRAID

I want to breathe with you
Unafraid
Never hold back
I want all of you
All of the time

Poems For My Wife

CREATION

You destroyed me
I only exist for you now
I will wrap my cock around you
A million times
Until you disappear
And when I do
You will feel the source of life
And know
I am your master
A love expressed in the nothingness of eternity
That awaits

IN THE VOID

I love you where there is nothing
In the void
Into something unknown
And I love you here
In this world
In this body
The way you move
The way you work and fuck
I feel your skin and the air around you
You suck my cock and know everything

GREECE

We danced at Classico
And the waiters danced too
We ate dinner at Nassau
That night
And I danced for you
With my hands
And the waiter said, "You like to dance."
We danced again
Outside the church on the hill
To the man playing his acoustic guitar
And the gypsy boy playing his accordion
Nearby

DILDO

I will lay you on the bed
And massage you
With that coconut oil I bought
Until you submit
To your deepest self

I LOVE YOU

I love you in your workout clothes
A mindless reptile body
Sweating and breathing and moving and smiling
You can't understand why I like you like this
Maybe it is the lady jogger we stopped
When I was little
Staring up at her heaving breasts and sweating hair
As she removed her yellow head phone to greet us

FLORIDA

I drove to Orlando
To pick you up
Skipped a meeting
We stayed at Havana Nights
I was in two hotels
Pretending to stay with the team
Would keep some clothes there
Run in at 6am and ruffle the sheets
But I was actually with you
At Havana Nights
Twenty minutes away
Up the stairs
To the right
In bed
Drinking a bottle of wine
From plastic cups

GO SLOW

I want you to suck my cock
In a place where cock sucking is an ancient language
Swimming through your underwater dream
Speak the language into me

UGANDA

There was no power
One day
And no water another
I made you mac and cheese
And we slept in the new bed I bought
With holes in the mosquito net
So you got bit
I took you to the airport
For the last time
No more airports
No more visits
Only long mornings
Doing what we are supposed to

YOUR MONSTER

A coat of arms
Eight feet tall
An empty black slit on my helmet
Staring at you
I am your monster to fuck
And be fucked by
Like a stranger
On a pinball machine

NOT ENOUGH

I want to kneel above you
And look down at your naked body
On the bed
You are my bread

MY HEART

I am warm
Tall
Naked
My chest is for you
My neck is for you
My stomach is for you
My legs are for you
My feet are for you
My back is for you
My hands are for you
My eyes are for you
My lips are for you
My hair is for you
My heart
Inside
Is for you

OUR STORY

They met at the Cowboy
She was friends with Jersey
He was friends with Lyon
She lived in Nashville
He lived in New York, in the house
Lyon and Jers said she was beautiful
The best
She came to the City for the weekend to see Jers
The two of them stood at the large kitchen counter drinking
She spoke loudly and inelegantly
Like a boy
Laughing selfishly
The next morning he could not believe
She was still speaking with nearly the same idiotic authority
What type of person could endure such a night unscathed

He wanted to impress her
Knew Lyon and Jers had probably said similar things about him
The best
He managed to tell a few stories
But thought she was mostly unconcerned

She felt the same
Wanted to know more
But was not troubled
Doubt was not her thing
She came from a family of farmers
Canadians
To them, sensitivity was useless
To be made hard, or better, vanish altogether

His family were Jews from the city
Sadness was nurtured
To them
Only the mind was useful

Sensitivity was valued above all
But they had the same feelings as kids that now
Powered their different constitutions as adults

For the New Year he went to Nashville to see everyone
Took a cab to her house late at night
It was raining
And they fucked
The bedroom door open
Liz talking to them from the kitchen

She spent her life this way, unburdened
Since nothing was wrong with her
Nothing was wrong with the world
Only peoples' decision kept them
From a similar perfection
In college, she swam
After college, she went into medical device sales
Making more money than the surgeons she took to dinner
Five nights a week
She rolled downhill
Collecting and flinging off bits along the way

He wavered
A ballplayer and a poet
Played in college and for years after
Playing for pennies to not have to grow up
For someone so lucky
The world had still managed to disappoint him
So to criticize and create a world
As good as the one he believed in as a boy
He made art
Wrote poems
Stories
Made paintings and music

They joined Liz for pizza
When they returned to the bedroom
They fucked again
And laughed the kind of laugh he had heard coming
From his parents' bedroom as a child

The next day, they stared at one another
Across a crowded room
Pretending to talk to other people
Distracted by their thumping chests
Secret smiles on their mouths
When they fucked that night
Something changed
There was a seriousness to it

He felt himself disappear
He no longer had needs of his own
Only wanted to please her
Fuck her
Explore with her
And in the way these things require a will
Then and there
He chose her
He saw a depth he hadn't noticed before
She could cross deserts while others wilted
She knew about the worlds that could be
She had not lost her childish instinct to be good
These things mattered to him
It did not hurt she was as beautiful as Lyon and Jers had said
Her body was smooth and powerful
He could stare into her large eyes and examine her face
Without shame

He was hard and soft at the same time
Big but weightless when he wrapped his arms around her
They enjoyed the rare privilege in life of being on the outside
Exactly as they felt on the inside

 Poems For My Wife

And now
Together
In the dark
They glowed

She saw his devotion and love
She knew
With him
She could have what she wanted

He whispered things like
Our stars are moving
I can feel it
Coaxing her closer
One word at a time
And she knew he was right
And in the way that these things require a will
Then and there
She chose him

And they lay together
Silently declaring their love
And animals of other worlds walked on air
In the sky
A million miles away
Their stars moved closer
Until they became one

www.ingramcontent.com/pod-product-compliance
Lightning Source LLC
Chambersburg PA
CBHW032133050726
47590CB00008B/3068